HOW TO WORK WITH STUPID PEOPLE

PEOPLE

A PRACTICAL GUIDE TO NAVIGATING WORKPLACE
CHALLENGES WITH STRATEGIC BUSINESS
COMMUNICATION SKILLS

JS PAXTON

SAGE

Cover design by Trillium Sage Publishing

ISBN: 978-1-958118-41-2 | ebook

ISBN: 978-1-958118-42-9 | paperback

CONTENTS

INTRODUCTION

After three excruciating decades of navigating the chaotic maze of stupidity in the workplace, I have seen it all. I have weathered inane conversations, battled irrational decisions, and endured meetings that make root canals seem enjoyable. The kind that brings about a headache before they enter the room. Yes, I have survived the onslaught of workplace stupidity, and now I want to pass these hard-won survival strategies on to you.

As a seasoned veteran in the biotech sector, I have been involved with teams across functions ranging from R&D to production, sales, and marketing. My career has afforded me the "pleasure" of collaborating with thousands of professionals over the years...and to say there's a wide spectrum of competencies would be an understatement. From the brilliant scientists advancing cutting-edge innovations to the oblivious marketers making baffling strategic moves, I've become well-acquainted with the menagerie of workplace stupidity.

While the majority of my colleagues have been talented, rational individuals, there is a special breed somehow gifted in the art of absurdity. These unique specimens possess a knack for convoluted thinking, illogical choices, and general workplace buffoonery. Their decision-making abilities seem to have gone on permanent vacation, often leaving others to deal with the frustrating aftermath. Beneath all of that, and at the end of it all, they are perfectly capable of tackling the task at hand.

In my earlier days, I'll admit dealing with such ineptitude often left me enraged and bitter. I would agonize over my powerlessness against the rising tide of stupid decisions threatening to drown our productivity. How could they not see the obvious flaws in their thinking? Why won't leadership listen to reason and logic? I would vent to my mentors, seeking advice on handling the relentless incompetence surrounding me. Their guidance proved invaluable over the years in maintaining my composure and learning to choose my battles.

Through determined practice and shifting my mindset, I gained the emotional tools to stay grounded when plunged into the chaos. I realized I had two choices – remain frustrated at the growing madness or hone strategies to navigate it. By focusing energy on the latter, I discovered certain techniques allow you to surface unscathed from even the most nonsensical situations. Instead of resisting stupidity, I learned to flow with it.

Now after years of trial-and-error combined with extensive behavioral research, I have compiled my hard-earned lessons into this definitive guide on dealing with workplace stupidity. Consider me your battle-weary mentor sharing tried and tested methods to help you survive the onslaught. I will uncover the different species of stupidity, dissect their perplexing psychology, and equip you with concrete tips to handle them.

You may be wondering...why even bother writing a book about stupid people? Can't I just avoid them? Well, unless you plan on living as a hermit, you will encounter these characters no matter your profession or workplace. Most of them are in disguise, too, with impressive resumés, and the right experience that you're looking for. Hoping they'll just go away is not a winning strategy! The only way forward is to build your awareness and develop proactive approaches tailored to each brand of stupidity. You can coexist with even the most bumbling colleague by understanding what makes them tick and adjusting your own responses. We can't control their behavior, but we can control how we react to them.

The pages ahead provide that very understanding along with actionable advice on maintaining your sanity amidst the madness. I cover everything from retaining composure in chaotic meetings to presenting convincing arguments when logic seems futile. You will learn how to decipher complex paperwork, make processes idiot-proof, and even find humor when things seem hopeless. I provide tips tailored to different work contexts, whether you are an executive attempting to steer strategy or an individual contributor trying to stay afloat. No matter where you find yourself in the corporate ecosystem, you will discover helpful ways of circumventing stupidity's negative impact.

While stupidity can be infuriating, I encourage cultivating empathy rather than contempt for such individuals. I know, I'm asking a lot of you, but stick with me here. Often their puzzling actions arise from psychological factors like insecurity, stubbornness or pressure rather than sheer ineptitude. By better understanding root causes, you can identify solutions that create positive change through guidance and support. Promoting intellectual growth benefits all.

So, welcome to your guide through the unconventional – yet inevitable – world of working with stupid people. Together we will tackle the mysteries behind their baffling behavior, find clarity amidst chaos, and emerge smarter and stronger from our voyage through the circus-like halls of absurdity. Just remember, no matter how incomprehensible things may seem, take comfort that you now have the tools and wisdom to prevail. Onward we go...into the depths of the madhouse!

CHAPTER 1

ENTER THE MADHOUSE

ake a gentle step into the wonderfully chaotic world of
working with stupid people. This is not a book for the faint
of heart or easily frustrated. No, this is a survival guide for those
brave souls who find themselves amid what we can only describe as
a madhouse. If any of what you read regarding the trademarks and
characteristics of stupid people sounds like your personal horo-
scope, then I am sorry to inform you that you just might be the
problem. However, keep reading! This book can still help you. I
hope.

As you read, keep in mind that I am not referring to people of a
lower intelligence. I am referring to perfectly capable people, with
all the intelligence required for the task at hand, who have characteristics or methods that are the opposite of productive. Those
who get in their own way and the way of others. The people
responsible for every delayed deadline, every late-night fix, and
every triple-length meeting.

These are the people who ask questions that have already been
answered a dozen times, who can't seem to grasp even the simplest
concepts, and who make choices that leave you scratching your

head in disbelief. They may possess titles and qualifications that would suggest otherwise, but their actions and decisions speak louder than any framed piece of paper hanging on their office wall.

Perhaps the most frustrating part of it all is that these people are *ju*st good enough at their jobs to stay. Casting them out entirely is not warranted, meaning you're stuck with them and the suffering they cause.

But fear not, you are not alone. Countless others have found themselves trapped in this madhouse, surrounded by stupidity at every corner. And that's where this book comes in. It is here to guide you, to offer you solace and strategies for navigating the labyrinth of idiocy.

In the chapters that follow, we will explore the different species of stupidity, helping you to identify the unique characteristics of each. From the Dreaded Oblivion Syndrome, where individuals seem blissfully unaware of their own incompetence, to the Stupid Decision-Making phenomena, where logic takes a vacation. We will cover it all. Help is on the way!

The Dreaded Oblivion Syndrome (DOS) is marked by a curious trait, where individuals possess an uncanny ability to remain completely unaware of their own incompetence. It's as if they exist in a blissful state of ignorance, immune to the reality of their shortcomings. How fun for them. They will persistently ask questions that have been answered countless times before or make statements that show a complete lack of understanding, leaving you wondering if they even pay attention. Engaging in conversations with these individuals can be a test of one's patience, as they exhibit unwavering confidence in their erroneous beliefs, often doubling down on their ignorance rather than acknowledging any potential mistakes. These kinds of people behave as if they are the only other person in the room. Recognizing the DOS is crucial in developing effective communication strategies, for dealing with these individuals requires patience, empathy, and perhaps a touch of humor. (Okay, slightly more than just a touch.)

The Stupid Decision-Making phenomenon is characterized by a knack for making choices that defy logic and rationale. Whether it's allocating precious resources to irrelevant projects, implementing convoluted processes that hinder efficiency, or brushing aside expert advice in favor of personal opinion, these individuals seem to possess an unerring ability to make the most baffling decisions. Engaging in discussions or attempting to sway their thinking can feel like shouting into a void, as they exhibit an unyielding stubbornness and an unreasonable attachment to their own misguided ideas. Those who suffer from this might also behave as if what they've done is a great favor to you, something worthy of winning a prize. Navigating the realm of Stupid Decision-Making requires not only adept communication skills but also finesse for presenting compelling arguments backed by data and evidence. The only trick is getting that information to settle within their stubborn minds. Thankfully, there is a trick to that.

To get there, we first need to ask a few questions. What lies beneath these manifestations of stupidity? Is there more to it than meets the eye? Are these individuals truly as foolish as they appear, or is there something deeper at play?

Psychologists and sociologists have long pondered the origins and nature of stupidity. Some argue that it stems from a lack of cognitive ability or intelligence. However, research shows that intelligence alone does not always correlate with wise decision-making or common sense. Stupidity is a multifaceted phenomenon, influenced by various factors, such as personality traits, biases, motivations, and even the environment in which individuals operate.

In his book *What Intelligence Tests Miss*, psychologist Keith Stanovich presents research showing that high IQ alone does not prevent poor real-world decision-making (Stanovich, 2009). He reveals a "knowledge-behavior gap" - smart people still act irrationally in certain situations. Specifically, Stanovich links obliviousness and irrational thinking to egocentrism and cognitive miserliness, the lazy tendency to default to effortless instead of analytic thinking. Thus, personality traits and biased thinking patterns undermine practical reasoning, disconnected from intelligence. This academic work robustly demonstrates the complex psychology linking obliviousness, irrationality, and egocentrism to flawed functioning despite high IQ.

One perspective suggests that stupidity can stem from a combination of arrogance and overconfidence. When individuals possess an inflated sense of their abilities, they may be more likely to overlook their shortcomings and ignore external feedback that challenges their beliefs. This arrogance can lead to a stubborn resistance to change or admitting mistakes, perpetuating a cycle of stupidity. It becomes a self-reinforcing behavior where individuals become blind to their own limitations and cannot recognize the impact their actions have on those around them.

An adding, contributing factor to stupidity is cognitive biases. These biases, such as confirmation bias or the tendency to seek information that confirms pre-existing beliefs, can cloud judgment and hinder critical thinking. Stupidity thrives in environments where diversity of thought is stifled, and alternative perspectives are dismissed or ignored. Unchallenged biases and a lack of open-mindedness can create an echo chamber of stupidity that perpetuates and reinforces irrational decision-making.

Organizational culture and workplace dynamics play a pivotal role in enabling or curbing stupidity. In toxic environments where blame and humiliation are the norm, fear reigns supreme, and individuals are discouraged from speaking up or challenging the status quo. Stupidity can flourish under these conditions as individuals prioritize self-preservation over sound decision-making. Organizations that foster psychological safety, encourage diverse opinions, and value critical thinking are better equipped to confront stupidity head-on, promoting a culture of intelligent decision-making and continuous improvement. However, making this change is never seamless. Stick around for the help you need if this is something you intend to take on.

Throughout this book, we will dive even deeper into the art of communication with the intellectually challenged, providing you with tips and tricks to ensure your message gets through, even when faced with a seemingly impenetrable wall of ignorance. We will analyze the psychology of these individuals' behaviors and provide insights on how to navigate and influence their actions. Our strategies will equip you to navigate through meetings that go on endlessly, wasting precious time on futile discussions. We'll also examine the maddening world of pointless paperwork, where bureaucratic procedures become a breeding ground for mind-numbing stupidity.

But amidst the chaos, there is hope. There are strategies you can employ to maintain your sanity and even escape the clutches of the stupidity trap. From setting clear boundaries to cultivating a sense of humor, we will explore methods for preserving your mental well-being while staying productive in the face of relentless stupidity. We will also discuss the importance of self-reflection, as it's crucial to assess our own actions and reactions when confronted with challenging situations. Understanding ourselves leads to clarity and the ability to navigate challenges with resilience and grace.

That being said, hold on tight and get ready for the ride of your professional career. Welcome to the madhouse. It'll be an adventure, filled with frustration, bewilderment, and perhaps even a few moments of triumph. The path forward may even seem a little unclear. However, in the next chapter, we will shed light on concrete strategies to decode complex behaviors and communicate effectively regardless of the irrationality you may encounter.

It's a lot to take in. So, before you move forward, let's recap the key takeaways from this section.

1. Prepare for frustration and bewilderment when working with irrational people.

Action step

Mentally brace yourself for challenging situations.

2. You will need to understand different types of stupidity, like the Dreaded Oblivion Syndrome and Stupid Decision Making.

Action step

Learn their characteristics to better respond.

3. Look beyond behaviors to root psychological causes like arrogance and bias.

Action step

Analyze underlying reasons for stupidity.

4. Tailor communication approaches to each brand of stupidity.

Action step

Use evidence and logic to sway oblivious people.

5. Foster critical thinking and psychological safety in your workplace.

Action step

Encourage diversity of thought and speaking up without fear.

CHAPTER 2

UNDERSTANDING THE DIFFERENT SPECIES OF STUPIDITY

W elcome to a comprehensive examination of the various species of stupidity you may encounter in your working life. Just like the rich tapestry of the natural world, the realm of human stupidity is a vast and diverse ecosystem, teeming with fascinating creatures. By understanding these different manifestations of stupidity, you will be better equipped to navigate the treacherous waters of the workplace.

Now, some of the worst cases might present more than one of these species within them. If that is the case, then I wish you luck, but I also believe in you. Take a look at the descriptions below to better understand the most frustrating of people that you deal with. Once you can understand the characteristics, you can move on to learning how to combat them.

The Oblivious Ostrich

This species of stupidity is characterized by its remarkable ability to bury its head in the sand, blissfully unaware of the chaos and confusion it creates. Oblivious Ostriches can often be found making contradictory statements, ignoring important information, or displaying a complete lack of awareness of their own incompetence.

Throughout this, they will be blissfully unaware of the increasingly frustrated tone in your voice, the fact that you're actually in an online meeting, or that you're on break. Head in the sand.

These individuals seem resistant to feedback and constructive criticism, often dismissing any attempt to rectify their mistakes. Despite evidence to the contrary, Oblivious Ostriches remain steadfast in their incorrect beliefs, causing frustration among their colleagues. Their lack of self-awareness can create roadblocks to progress and hinder the efficiency of any collaborative endeavor.

To deal with an Oblivious Ostrich, patience and clear communication are key. Presenting evidence and facts in a manner that is not confrontational can help to gradually raise their awareness and promote a more enlightened approach to problem-solving. Developing strategies to provide them with increased exposure to diverse perspectives and experiences can broaden their understanding and challenge their preconceived notions. The key is to inch their heads out of the sand slowly, making sure that they are supported along the way. It's bright outside of that hole, and they might not like it.

With the correct guidance, they can find their own way and you can save yourself the battle.

The Bumbling Buffalo

Next, we'll discuss the individuals who possess an innate talent for turning even the simplest task into a bewildering ordeal. Whether it's fumbling with technology, misplacing critical documents, or asking redundant questions, the Bumbling Buffalo always finds a way to inject a dose of confusion into any situation. A Bumbling Buffalo might even take something as simple as a coffee run and turn it into a marathon. What's worse? They'll take you with them. Bumbling Buffalos are often accompanied by casualties, those drawn into the chaos.

Bumbling Buffalos often struggle with basic organizational skills, leading to inefficiencies and unnecessary frustrations for themselves and their colleagues. The Bumbling Buffalo's lack of attention to detail and poor time management can cause missed deadlines and sloppy work. Bumbling Buffalos might forget about a task or deadline entirely. Their calendars do not look like ours, I can promise you that.

Sometimes, and rather ironically, a Bumbling Buffalo creates chaos in their wake through their attempts at being more efficient. They'll adopt a code within their to-do list in order to take notes faster, only to not understand the code later, causing confusion when it comes time to take on the task.

When working alongside a Bumbling Buffalo, it is crucial to offer guidance and support without undermining their confidence. Establishing simple processes, providing step-by-step instructions, and encouraging them to ask for help when needed can help mitigate their impact. By fostering an open and supportive environment, Bumbling Buffalos can be nudged towards improvement and become valuable contributors to the team. Providing opportunities for them to enhance their organizational and time management skills can help them thrive in their roles. At the end, Bumbling Buffalos, by nature, can juggle a lot. If their processes can be streamlined or managed better, they can become an incredibly effective member of a team.

 *Quick Note*

To effectively handle stupid people, it is essential to try to understand how their minds work. Though their thinking may seem completely irrational, there is often an underlying logic and motivation behind their bizarre actions. For example, a Bumbling Buffalo might reorganize their desktop before starting an enormous project. They are attempting to make what they need easier to find. However, their attempts might be too extreme, and when the time comes, they can't remember their new filing system, ultimately causing delays.

Start by asking yourself - what insecurities might drive their behavior? Stupid people often mask deep feelings of inadequacy through misplaced confidence and stubbornness. Their extreme reactions may stem from feeling threatened or afraid of being viewed as incapable. Is there a culture of competition within your workplace? To some, that might cause added and unnecessary stress, resulting in odd choices and behaviors.

Similarly, explore what biases might cloud their judgment. We all have selective perceptions and draw faulty conclusions based on limited perspectives. Stupid people simply lack the self-awareness to recognize these pitfalls in their thinking. Also, examine environmental factors that reward and thus reinforce stupidity. Sometimes incompetent bosses or toxic work cultures perpetuate flawed reasoning by failing to challenge it.

Dig into why stupid people resist change and learning so vehemently. Growth requires vulnerability and admitting imperfections, which can intensely discomfort those with fragile egos and false self-perceptions. By analyzing root psychological causes, situational influences, and the internal logic of stupid people, we gain invaluable insights to guide our responses to them. Bumbling Buffalos are perfectly capable, they simply require a different approach to others in the workplace.

The Teflon Tactician

This next breed of stupidity is known for its impressive skill at deflecting responsibility and deflecting blame. No matter how glaringly obvious their errors may be, the Teflon Tactician has an uncanny ability to avoid taking ownership. Instead, they possess an arsenal of strategies, such as finger-pointing, playing the victim, or conveniently forgetting crucial details.

Teflon Tacticians excel at shifting blame onto others, skillfully evading accountability for their actions. Their behavior undermines trust and can lead to a toxic work environment, where conflicts escalate, and problems go unresolved. It is essential to address this type of stupidity promptly to maintain a healthy and productive team dynamic.

To counteract the Teflon Tactician's tactics, it is crucial to establish transparency and create a culture of accountability. Promote a safe environment where open discussions about mistakes and their consequences are encouraged. When giving honest feedback about mistakes, it's important to avoid harsh reactions that could diminish openness. Rather, make it seem like the right thing to do, something to be proud of.

Building strong relationships and fostering a sense of shared responsibility can help dismantle the Teflon Tactician's deflection mechanisms, ultimately leading to a more effective and harmonious workplace. Providing training and resources on conflict resolution and effective communication can aid in addressing underlying issues that contribute to their behavior.

Teflon Tacticians need to be addressed early on as they can create trouble within a workplace, and especially within a team. They have an innate ability to take something functioning and disrupt it with their tactics. If you find yourself with a Teflon Tactician on your team, I suggest you take action immediately. They will sour those who were previously happy workers, and nobody can afford to take that risk.

Thankfully, while they can be the most dangerous kind of stupid to have in the workplace, they can be managed. There is something that can be done. So, if you're reading this, and someone you know fits this description, take a deep breath. It will be alright.

The Drone of Drudgery

These individuals are masters of mind-numbing repetition. They approach their work with a robotic monotony, showing no inclination for efficiency, innovation, or critical thinking. The Drone of Drudgery is content to follow the same outdated processes year after year, blissfully ignorant of any improvements made in the industry.

These individuals resist change and often lack initiative, stifling progress within the organization. Their inability to adapt or seek more efficient methods can leave them and their colleagues stuck in a cycle of mediocrity.

Addressing this type of stupidity requires fostering a growth mindset and encouraging continuous learning. Starting open discussions about industry advancements, offering opportunities for professional development, and highlighting successful instances of innovation can inspire Drones of Drudgery to break free from their entrenched ways and embrace new possibilities.

Providing them with a platform to share their expertise and encouraging them to explore different ways of approaching their work can help uncover hidden talents and interests that may have been stifled. Always make it fun. Drones of Drudgery have lost their inspiration to change or to adapt. Doing it the same way as always is simply too easy to let go of. They need a new spark before they'll be willing to try a fresh approach.

The Jargon Juggler

This breed of stupidity manifests itself through the excessive use of buzzwords, corporate jargon, and incomprehensible acronyms. The Jargon Juggler skillfully weaves together long-winded sentences laden with terms like 'synergy', 'leverage', and 'paradigm shift', often leaving their listeners struggling to decipher their intended meaning. They can take a five-minute presentation and turn it into a thirty-minute presentation. Often, they'll prefer quantity over quality, believing that the more important it *sounds*, the more important it *is*.

Jargon Jugglers use confusing jargon as a shield, disguising their lack of expertise or substance behind a veil of linguistic complexity. They may come across as intellectuals, but in reality, they muddy the waters and hinder effective communication. Nobody can keep up with them, and they struggle to get to the point. This can cause frustration on many levels, particularly if those who come into contact with such a person are on a tight schedule.

To combat the Jargon Juggler's impact, it is crucial to establish clear communication guidelines within the workplace. Encourage a culture of simplicity and clarity, promoting straightforward and jargon-free language. In meetings or discussions, politely request clarification whenever jargon is used, highlighting the importance of effective communication for a productive work environment.

Providing training on effective communication techniques and promoting active listening can help minimize misunderstandings and improve overall clarity in workplace interactions. You will need to prove to the Jargon Juggler that they still sound smart without their jargon.

The Frenzied Firefighter

Akin to a chicken running around with its head cut off, the Frenzied Firefighter thrives on creating crises and then frantically attempting to put them out. This species of stupidity is known for its inability to prioritize, constantly jumping from one urgent matter to another without a clear understanding of what is truly important or deserving of immediate attention. Or, quite commonly also, they will make every task a matter of priority.

Their scattered approach to work often leads to burnout, missed deadlines, and a lack of focus. The Frenzied Firefighter's reactive mindset prevents effective planning and hampers long-term strategic thinking. Why do they do it? From a misguided idea of what it takes to be important in the workplace.

The Frenzied Firefighter might be under the impression that those who are always busy are important. Or seems important. If they want to feel more important in the workplace, they might create chaos for themselves and save the day later. That way, they are justified within their field of expertise. It's Hero Syndrome in the workplace, and it can be a dangerous thing to deal with.

To help the Frenzied Firefighter regain control, emphasize the importance of prioritization and time management. Provide tools and resources to help organize tasks, set realistic deadlines, and outline clear objectives. Encourage them to adopt a proactive approach, breaking down tasks into manageable steps, and focusing on the most critical elements first.

Promoting a culture of work-life balance and stress management can help ease the frenzied behavior by supporting overall well-being and fostering a more measured, thoughtful approach to work.

With that, you now clearly understand the kind of stupid you might be dealing with.

Understanding these different species of stupidity is crucial in your endeavor to work more effectively with your colleagues. By recognizing the characteristics and behaviors associated with each species, you will be better equipped to expect their actions and implement strategies to mitigate their negative impact on your work environment.

Remember, the goal is not to belittle or mock these individuals but rather to develop strategies for working alongside them. With patience, tact, and a healthy dose of humor, you may find that even the most challenging situations can be navigated with relative ease. At the end, you'll likely find yourself with a perfectly competent and necessary addition to your team. That's something to look forward to!

Now that we have explored the techniques needed to interpret and navigate absurd behaviors, we must prioritize self-care when faced with workplace frustration. Coming up, we will discuss various methods to safeguard your mental well-being and find meaning amidst the madness.

Before then, here's one last note from this chapter.

Economic historian Carlo Maria Cipolla, known for his studies on human stupidity like *The Basic Laws of Human Stupidity*, lists these five rules of stupidity (Principia Scientific Intl., 2021):

THE FIVE FUNDAMENTAL LAWS OF STUPIDITY

1. Always and inevitably, each of us underestimates the number of stupid individuals in the world.
2. The probability that a certain person is stupid is independent of any other characteristic of the same person.
3. A stupid person is one who causes harm to another person or group without at the same time getting a benefit for himself or even damaging himself.
4. Non-stupid people always underestimate the harmful potential of stupid people.
5. The stupid person is the most dangerous person who exists.

Here is your recap and key takeaways for understanding the different species of stupid:

The Oblivious Ostrich

1. Remain patient and keep communication clear when providing feedback.

2. Present facts and data to gradually raise self-awareness.

3. Expose them to diverse perspectives to challenge assumptions.

4. Don't take their confidence personally. Insecurity drives the oblivion.

5. Roadblocks stem from their lack of self-awareness, not incompetence.

The Bumbling Buffalo

1. Offer guidance without undermining their confidence.

2. Provide step-by-step instructions to mitigate confusion.

3. Encourage asking questions to reduce mistakes.

4. Establish clear processes and deadlines.

5. Build time management and organizational skills.

The Teflon Tactician

1. Promote a culture of accountability and ownership.

2. Address deflection tactics promptly yet tactfully.

3. Encourage open discussions about consequences.

4. Foster shared responsibility within teams.

5. Provide conflict resolution and communication training.

The Drone of Drudgery

1. Initiate discussions on innovations in the field.

2. Offer continuous learning and development opportunities.

3. Highlight examples of progress made through change.

4. Give them a platform to share their expertise.

5. Uncover hidden talents by encouraging alternative approaches.

The Jargon Juggler

1. Establish clear communication guidelines.

2. Promote a culture focused on simplicity.

3. Request clarification when jargon causes confusion.

4. Provide training on effective communication.

5. Encourage active listening in interactions.

The Frenzied Firefighter

1. Emphasize prioritization and time management.

2. Provide tools to organize tasks and set deadlines.

3. Encourage a proactive rather than reactive approach.

4. Promote work-life balance and stress management.

5. Break large goals down into manageable steps.

CHAPTER 3

EMBRACING YOUR INNER ZEN AND PRIORITIZING SELF-CARE

W orking with stupid people can be mentally exhausting and emotionally draining. It often feels like a never-ending endurance task that tests your patience and sanity. Finding inner peace and maintaining a sense of serenity becomes paramount. While it may seem like an uphill battle, fear not, for within the depths of your being lies the power to embrace your inner Zen and find tranquility amidst the chaos. It's crucial to prioritize your well-being in order to navigate this challenging environment successfully. If you find yourself struggling, tag the most relevant parts of this book and refer back to it as often as required. If that doesn't work, there's always wine.

In this chapter, we will discuss various self-care techniques that can help you maintain your sanity amidst the chaos.

Acceptance

Begin your journey towards achieving Zen-like serenity by embracing the reality of working with people of varying intelligence levels and capabilities. In accepting this truth, you open yourself up to a world of empathy and appreciation for the diverse range of personalities and skill sets that exist in your workplace. Each individual, no matter their intellectual capacity, brings something unique to the table. This is achieved by understanding the characteristics outlined in Chapter 2. Be sure to know what you're up against so that you can anticipate anything that might be thrown your way.

Letting Go of Control

Trying to control the actions and behavior of others is a futile endeavor that only leads to frustration and disappointment. Redirect your energy to controlling how you react and respond. Let go of the need to constantly intervene or correct the mistakes of your colleagues. Detach yourself emotionally from their actions and remind yourself that their shortcomings are not a reflection of your own worth or abilities. When they do the right thing, make sure that they know about it. Make it easier on yourself, by making it worth their while.

Establish Boundaries

One of the most critical aspects of self-care when dealing with difficult people is establishing clear boundaries. This involves setting limits on how much of your time, energy, and emotional resources you are willing to invest in their problematic behavior. By defining and communicating these boundaries, you protect yourself from being overwhelmed and maintain a sense of control over your own well-being. This might involve learning to say no, setting realistic expectations, and consciously disconnecting from work-related concerns during your personal time. This task will never be a quick one. Tackling frustrating and stupid people in the workplace takes time. So, don't expect too much too soon, and be kind to yourself.

.   .   .

Practice Patience

Faced with idiocy, patience is truly a virtue. Take a deep breath before reacting to nonsensical remarks or actions. Remind yourself that patience is not a sign of weakness, but a testament to your resilience and self-control. Cultivate the ability to remain calm and composed, no matter how absurd the situation may be. Understand that impatience only breeds more impatience and does not serve any productive purpose. Be an example of what it is you're looking for. Patience is your one true chance at surviving this.

Seek Solitude

Amidst the tumultuousness of the world, find solace in moments of solitude. Regularly carve out brief breaks throughout the day to clear your mind and recharge. Step outside and go for a walk, find a quiet place to think, or practice calming techniques like deep breathing or meditation. These minor acts can have a profound effect on restoring your inner calm. Embrace the power of silence and observe how it allows you to reconnect with your true self, away from the noise and distractions of the outside world.

 A note from the trenches

In my early consulting days, I remember being confused when the marketing director presented our "visionary" growth strategy in a 52-slide deck. I could feel my frustration building as he scanned through bizarre photos, illogical charts, and outlandish concepts.

As my frustration grew, I excused myself for a restroom break. I remembered that losing my cool in front of the leadership team would not be good for anyone. I pictured myself in a peaceful environment, blissfully unaware of the absurd presentation. After a few minutes, I felt better and could return to the meeting. Despite my frustration, I concentrated on practical solutions rather than emotional responses. When these situations arise, I have to remember to use these grounding strategies to restore calm and protect my sanity!

- DG

Find Humor in the Absurd

Finding humor amid workplace absurdities can serve as an invaluable coping mechanism. When faced with mind-bogglingly absurd situations, take a step back to appreciate the comedy of it all rather than let frustration set in. Allow yourself to revel in the ridiculousness. However, take care that your comedy lacks callousness. Laugh with colleagues in a balanced way that maintains professionalism, perspective, and supportive relationships. Enjoy the absurdity of it all. (Just a little bit.)

Cultivate Empathy

While it may be tempting to dismiss your colleagues as hopelessly unintelligent, take a moment to consider their perspectives and challenges. Cultivating empathy allows you to see beyond their shortcomings and understand that everyone has their strengths and weaknesses. Put yourself in their shoes and imagine the difficulties they face. By fostering a sense of understanding, you create an environment of compassion and tolerance, which can help mitigate the negative impact of working with intellectually challenged individuals.

.   .   .

Engage in Self-Reflection

When confronted with stupidity, it is essential to engage in self-reflection to better understand your reactions and responses. Take the time to analyze patterns of behavior or triggers that exacerbate your frustration. By gaining insight into your own emotional landscape, you can develop strategies to cope more effectively. Journaling, seeking therapy, or discussing your thoughts and emotions with trusted individuals can prove immensely valuable in examining your own responses and identifying healthier coping mechanisms. I know what you're thinking. Can't the other person do that? They could, but you shouldn't expect them to. That will only lead to further frustration. Rely on yourself through this.

Prioritize Self-Care Activities

Faced with ongoing challenges, prioritizing self-care becomes paramount. Engage in activities that rejuvenate and restore your energy levels. Whether it's regular physical exercise to release tension, pursuing a hobby that brings you joy, spending quality time with loved ones who offer support, or simply enjoying a hot bath to unwind, investing time in self-care is essential. Experiment with different practices to find what resonates with you and ensure consistency in incorporating them into your daily or weekly routine. Consistent self-care replenishes your mental and emotional reserves, enabling you to navigate the challenges at work with greater resilience and balance.

If you've had a particularly tough day, and those without have stolen your brain cells from you.

Here are simple self-care ideas for a quick break in the workplace, should you be stuck on what to do next:

Take a short walk outside to get some fresh air and sunlight

Do some seated stretches or yoga poses at your desk

Drink a full glass of water to stay hydrated

Eat a healthy snack like fruit, vegetables, or nuts

Listen to an uplifting playlist or podcast episode

Take 5 deep breaths, focusing on your inhales and exhales

Do a quick meditation or body scan

Make yourself a warm herbal tea

Write in a gratitude journal

Take a power nap or just close your eyes for 5 minutes

Go chat with a co-worker you enjoy spending time with

Look at an inspirational quote or cute picture that makes you smile

Declutter one section of your desk to feel more focused
Step outside and look up at the clouds

Write down 3 things you have accomplished recently

Take an online mini-workout break

Slowly eat a piece of your favorite candy or chocolate

Take a quick solo dance break to your favorite upbeat song

Spend three minutes doing mindful coloring

Call or text a loved one

Massage pressure points on your hands and wrists

Watch a funny YouTube video

Compliment three people around you

Set your next attainable goal

Water your office plants

Sketch something creative like an abstract design

Tell yourself an affirmation (or listen to an affirmation audio book) to lift your spirits

Focus on the Bigger Picture

When frustrated, step back and focus on your long-term goals instead of immediate challenges. Ask yourself: What do you truly value? What are your long-term ambitions? Concentrate your energy on personal growth and development by maintaining a clear vision of what truly matters to you. By keeping the bigger picture in mind, you can maintain perspective, reduce the impact of others' incompetence on your own well-being, and set an example for those around you. Do not make managing the surrounding stupidity the most important part of your day. You are not being fair to yourself then. Make it a long-term goal with short-term steps. After all, you still have to meet your deadlines.

. . .

Find a Support Network

It can feel isolating and frustrating when dealing with stupidity, but you are not alone in this struggle. Building relationships with colleagues who understand your challenges can provide a supportive network where you can freely express your frustrations and seek advice or validation. Engaging with like-minded individuals who share your experiences can offer comfort and relief as you realize others face similar difficulties. Seek allies in your workplace who can offer a fresh perspective on dealing with stupidity and provide solidarity in navigating challenging situations. Outside of work, cultivate relationships with mentors or trusted friends who can offer objective advice and support, reminding you of your worth beyond the obstacles you encounter.

Adopt Mindfulness Practices

Mindfulness techniques can be powerful tools for maintaining your sanity when faced with stupidity. Engaging in practices such as meditation, deep breathing exercises, or even just taking moments of intentional stillness can help you stay grounded amidst the chaos. These activities help you redirect your focus from external chaos to internal clarity. By training your mind to focus on the present moment and observe your thoughts and emotions non-judgmentally, you create space for yourself to respond consciously rather than reactively. Regular practice of mindfulness can equip you with the ability to recognize frustration and stress as they arise, enabling you to respond with clarity and compassion.

The most important thing to remember is that embracing your inner Zen and practicing self-care is a profound and ongoing process. It requires dedication, self-reflection, and a genuine commitment to personal growth. As you embark on this transformative journey, remember that the power to find peace amidst the chaos of idiocy lies within you. By adopting these strategies and forging a deeper connection with your inner self, you can navigate the challenges of working with intellectually challenged individuals with grace, patience, and an unwavering sense of serenity. Prioritizing your mental well-being and your pursuit of Zen allows you to not only maintain your sanity but also thrive in the face of adversity. Your personal well-being also creates a ripple effect, positively influencing those around you and fostering a more harmonious and mindful work environment.

Before we move on, let's recap this chapter:

1. Accept the reality of working with people of varying capabilities.

Action step

Embrace empathy and appreciation for the diverse range of skills.

2. Let go of trying to control others' behaviors.

Action step

Focus your energy on controlling your own reactions and responses.

3. Establish clear boundaries on your time and emotional investment.

Action step

Learn to say no, set expectations, and disconnect after work hours.

4. Cultivate patience through deep breaths and self-talk.

Action step

Remind yourself frustration serves no purpose and patience shows resilience.

5. Seek solitude through quiet breaks.

Action step

Step outside, meditate, or take a few minutes of stillness to clear your mind and restore calm.

CHAPTER 4
DEALING WITH THE DREADED OBLIVION SYNDROME

I n this chapter, we learn about the mind-boggling phenomenon we like to call the Dreaded Oblivion Syndrome (DOS). Picture this: you're in a meeting, trying to discuss an important project, and there's that one person who seems completely unaware of what's going on. They ask irrelevant questions, repeat what others have said, or simply sit there in a daze, lost in their own world. I get it, it's incredibly frustrating. It lengthens every meeting and can cause irreparable tears in concentration levels. In this chapter, I'm going to equip you with the tools to navigate this baffling condition.

It's essential to understand that the DOS sufferer is not intentionally trying to be difficult. They genuinely lack awareness of their surroundings and struggle to comprehend the information being presented. Empathy is key here. Resist the urge to roll your eyes or sigh. Remember, they didn't ask to be afflicted by DOS. The last thing you want to do is let them know you find them annoying. This will only make them more self-conscious, leading to further DOS behavior.

To cope with someone experiencing DOS, employ the art of clear and concise communication. Keep your explanations simple, use visual aids if possible, and break down complex ideas into smaller, digestible parts. This will help the DOS sufferer grasp the core concept without feeling overwhelmed. Where necessary, ask that questions be kept until the end so that you have the chance to potentially answer them along the way. This eliminates further disruptions.

Try to further create an environment that minimizes distractions. Ensure the meeting room is well-lit, free from excessive noise, and devoid of unnecessary visual stimuli. By reducing external disruptions, you can help the DOS sufferer better focus on the matter at hand.

Patience is your greatest ally when grappling with DOS. Reinforce their understanding by asking open-ended questions that encourage them to think critically. This approach allows them to engage and contribute positively to the discussion without feeling singled out or inadequate. It will boost their confidence, ultimately ending the unnecessary additions to the conversation.

Sometimes, it may be necessary to gently redirect the conversation to keep it on track. Try skillfully steering the discussion back towards the primary goal or agenda item, ensuring that no one is left stranded in the abyss of the DOS sufferer's tangents.

If all else fails and DOS shows no signs of dissipating, consider seeking support from a higher authority. Share your concerns with a supervisor, manager, or human resources department, outlining the challenges caused by DOS. They may provide alternative strategies or resources, such as additional training or mentoring, to help the individual overcome their obliviousness.

Where DOS seems pervasive, it may be worthwhile to explore whether underlying factors contribute to the condition. For instance, some individuals may struggle with attention deficit disorders or cognitive impairments that affect their ability to follow conversations or absorb information. By recognizing these underlying causes, you can adopt a more compassionate and tailored approach to support their needs.

Taking a step back, let us consider the impact of DOS on the individual themselves. Imagine being trapped in a perpetual state of confusion, constantly feeling like an outsider trying to navigate a world of intricate details and unfathomable concepts. The frustration and self-doubt they experience can be demoralizing. Offering support, encouragement, and understanding can make a significant difference in their daily life, beyond just the confines of the meeting room.

Always keep in mind that the DOS sufferer is clueless to how their behavior impacts the rest of those present. So, responding in a way that lets them know you're annoyed is detrimental. Those who suffer from DOS might take it personally, which might make them feel like they need to try harder, which might lead to further distraction, further pointless questions, and an unending cycle.

Addressing DOS requires a delicate balance, as overcompensating or treating the individual as incompetent can be equally damaging. Respect their intellect and abilities while using targeted interventions to bridge any gaps in understanding. Offering constructive feedback, subtle cues, and gentle reminders can help prevent DOS from obstructing progress, and ultimately empower the individual to reach their full potential.

Perhaps most importantly, remember to maintain your own sanity throughout the ordeal. DOS can test even the most patient souls, so be sure to practice self-care. Take breaks when needed, vent your frustrations healthily, and seek comfort in the camaraderie of colleagues who can sympathize with your struggle.

By staying calm, employing effective communication strategies, seeking support when necessary, and understanding the potential underlying factors contributing to DOS, you can navigate the treacherous waters of Dreaded Oblivion Syndrome. With time and perseverance, you may even unintentionally become an advocate for awareness and inclusion, spreading understanding about DOS and fostering an environment that supports individual differences.

The time has come to break free from the confines of a stagnated work life. In the next chapter will provide the keys to escape the vortex of stupidity and embark on a journey toward greater fulfillment guided by your inner brilliance.

Don't forget what you've learned in this chapter:

1. Practice empathy rather than frustration towards those with obliviousness or confusion.

Action step

Remember they do not choose this condition and also face challenges.

2. Use clear communication and break down information.

Action step

Present ideas in smaller chunks with visual aids.

3. Minimize external distractions for better focus.

Action step

Ensure the environment has minimal disruptions and stimuli.

4. Ask thoughtful questions to promote engagement and critical thinking.

Action step

Pose open-ended questions that encourage analysis.

5. Explore potential underlying causes, like disorders or impairments.

Action step

Adopt a compassionate approach if specific needs exist.

CHAPTER 5

STRATEGIES FOR COMMUNICATING WITH THE INTELLECTUALLY CHALLENGED

U nlike previous chapters focusing on the arrogant and close-minded, here we address communicating with those who might actually be intellectually challenged. In these situations, I'd like to encourage you to recognize cognitive limitations with empathy, not frustration. The goal is to foster dignity and inclusion through understanding. We will explore strategies to effectively connect with intellectually challenged individuals in a sensitive, empowering way. Mastering this can be life-changing.

Use Clear and Simple Language

Intellectually challenged individuals may face difficulties with comprehension, so it is vital to use clear and simple language when communicating with them. Avoid using complex terminology or abstract concepts that could confuse or overwhelm them. Instead, focus on using straightforward and concise language. If the intellectual challenge comes in the form of perpetual overthinking, then clear communication can help put their minds at ease.

Break down information into smaller, more easily digestible pieces that they can grasp. Providing concrete examples and familiar analogies related to their experiences can aid in their understanding and promote clarity. Allow them the chance to be confident they understand what you're saying.

Practice Patience and Empathy

Patience and empathy are paramount when communicating with intellectually challenged individuals. Remember that they may require additional time to process and absorb information. Avoid rushing them or displaying frustration, as this could impede their learning experience. Instead, take a relaxed and understanding approach, allowing them the necessary time to understand and respond. Empathy plays a crucial role in building trust and rapport; try to put yourself in their shoes, appreciating the challenges they face, and offering support accordingly. Be a mentor and set an example of the behavior you would like them to adopt.

Use Visual Aids and Multimedia Tools

Everyone has a different way of learning. For some, visual aids can greatly enhance understanding and bridge gaps in comprehension. By utilizing diagrams, charts, pictures, or other visual representations, you can provide additional support for conveying your message. Visual aids serve as visual references that can be easier to grasp than verbal or written explanations alone, making them an invaluable tool for effective communication. Consider incorporating multimedia tools such as videos or interactive presentations that engage multiple senses and facilitate learning through different modalities. The more support you can provide for communication, the better.

Active Listening and Non-Verbal Communication

Active listening plays a fundamental role in effective communication with intellectually challenged individuals. Give them your full attention, maintain eye contact, and acknowledge their contributions. Avoid interrupting or finishing their sentences. By actively listening, you show respect and create a supportive environment that encourages them to share their thoughts and concerns. Practice reflective listening by paraphrasing their statements to ensure you understand their perspective fully. This not only helps clarify any misunderstandings but also communicates empathy and validation. Pay attention to non-verbal cues, as individuals with intellectual challenges might struggle to express their thoughts verbally. Body language, facial expressions, and gestures can provide valuable insights into their feelings and level of engagement. Part of their frustration could stem from their inability to choose the right words or have the correct vocabulary. Hear them out when they ramble, so that you can give them a chance to express themselves. Pay attention to their mannerisms as they speak, they might gesture what they actually mean. This will provide help and clarity on both ends, creating a more positive experience for all.

Adapt Your Communication Style and Modulate Delivery

Intellectually challenged individuals may respond differently to various communication styles, making adaptability key. Pay close attention to their unique preferences and adjust your approach accordingly. Some individuals may benefit from a visual approach, where pictures or written instructions are more effective than verbal explanations. Others may respond well to repetition or the use of metaphors, which can simplify complex concepts. Modulate the tone and pace of your speech to ensure clarity and avoid overwhelming them with information. By flexibly adapting your communication style, you can tailor your interactions to suit their needs.

Provide Feedback and Encouragement

Regular feedback and encouragement play a crucial role in effective communication. Praise and positive reinforcement are powerful motivators, especially when individuals understand or accomplish a task. Celebrate their achievements, no matter how small, to boost their self-confidence and promote a sense of accomplishment. Constructive feedback can also be useful in clarifying misunderstandings and suggesting alternative approaches, provided the feedback is delivered with empathy and respect. Provide specific guidance for further development while highlighting strengths and areas for improvement to balance your feedback.

Cultivate a Supportive and Inclusive Environment

Creating a supportive and inclusive environment goes beyond individual communication strategies. Foster an atmosphere that values diversity and respects the unique abilities and challenges of intellectually challenged individuals. Encourage team members and peers to embrace inclusive practices and develop a sense of belonging. Collaborate with support networks, such as family members, caregivers, or specialists, to ensure consistent and effective communication approaches across different settings.

Effective communication with intellectually challenged individuals requires empathy, understanding, and a willingness to adapt your communication style. By implementing these strategies, you can foster an environment that encourages open dialogue, understanding, and empowerment.

Before we move on, remember:

1. Use clear, simple language and break down information into digestible pieces.

Action step

Avoid complex terminology and abstract concepts. Focus on concise, straightforward communication.

2. Practice patience and empathy when communicating.

Action step

Allow additional time for them to process information without rushing or showing frustration.

3. Incorporate visual aids and multimedia tools.

Action step

Use diagrams, charts, and videos to provide additional support.

4. Actively listen and pay attention to non-verbal cues.

Action step

Maintain eye contact, avoid interrupting them, and observe body language and facial expressions.

5. Adapt your communication style to their needs and preferences.

Action step

Be flexible in tailoring your tone, pace, and approach based on what engages them best.

CHAPTER 6

STUPID DECISION-MAKING 101: WHEN LOGIC JUMPS OUT THE WINDOW

I n a world full of intelligent people, you'd think that decision-making would be a breeze. But alas, the universe delights in throwing us curveballs in the form of stupid decision-makers. So, how does one navigate this maze of illogical choices and mind-boggling actions? Get ready for Stupid Decision-Making 101, where we'll explore this peculiar phenomenon and arm you with the best strategies to survive.

Understanding the Stupidity Spectrum

In order to effectively navigate the land of stupid decision-making, it is crucial to recognize the different levels that exist on the stupidity spectrum. This spectrum ranges from mild confusion to full-blown idiocy, with varying degrees of illogical thinking and flawed perceptions. By familiarizing ourselves with the different stages of the spectrum, we can better assess the situation at hand and adjust our approach accordingly.

Mild Confusion

This stage involves individuals who may be slightly misguided or misinformed in their decision-making process. They may lack the necessary knowledge or critical thinking skills to make logical choices. They might have a hard time remembering all the details or simply have no process for good planning strategies. In such cases, gentle guidance and education can help steer them towards more rational decisions. Implementing better processes and clearer guidelines will be imperative. However, it's important to approach these situations with empathy and not dismiss their concerns or belittle their perspectives.

Deliberate Ignorance

Moving a step further on the stupidity spectrum, we encounter individuals who intentionally ignore or deny facts and evidence, often driven by personal biases or hidden agendas. Dealing with such individuals requires a delicate balance of presenting facts, challenging their misconceptions, and fostering open-mindedness. It may be useful to appeal to their values or goals to find common ground, allowing for a more productive conversation. Always keep an open mind when working with someone who displays deliberate ignorance. It is important never to judge. Starting off on the right foot when it comes to trust matters in dealing with someone who shows deliberate ignorance.

Utter Foolishness

At the extreme end of the spectrum, we have individuals who consistently make irrational decisions with no logical basis. They seem to possess an innate talent for disregarding even the most basic principles of reason. Handling such situations can be incredibly challenging, requiring careful consideration of alternative approaches to guide them toward more sensible choices. In such cases, it may be necessary to involve mediators or authorities to intervene and provide objective guidance.

ANALYZING THE ANATOMY OF A STUPID DECISION

In order to move forward in the process, we need to dive headfirst into dissecting the thought process (if any) behind a stupid decision. We'll resolve the mysteries of logic jumping out the window, as we examine the key factors contributing to irrational choices. By understanding the underlying thought patterns, you'll be better equipped to respond efficiently.

Emotional Reasoning

Stupid decisions often arise from an over-reliance on emotions rather than facts and rational thinking. Emotions can cloud judgment, leading individuals to prioritize short-term gratification over long-term consequences. By recognizing this tendency, we can work towards encouraging a more balanced approach that embraces both emotional intelligence and logical reasoning.

Cognitive Biases

Humans are susceptible to various cognitive biases that can derail decision-making. Confirmation bias, for instance, leads people to seek information that supports their existing beliefs while ignoring contradictory evidence (MSEd, 2022). Understanding biases and consciously challenging them can help mitigate their influence on decision-making processes. Listed below are seven types of biases and ways to work through them (Gould, 2023).

Confirmation Bias

Confirmation bias is the tendency to seek out and accept information that confirms our existing beliefs while ignoring or dismissing facts that contradict them, which can reinforce false ideas if we fail to consider other viewpoints. One sign of confirmation bias is only pursuing supporting evidence for our beliefs while avoiding or rationalizing away contradictory information, which closes our minds to truth and reflects poorly on our judgment. Overcoming confirmation bias requires consciously seeking facts that challenge our perspectives along with asking others to critique our positions in order to test them against reality.

Attribution Bias

Attribution bias causes one to view others' behaviors as intentionally motivated by inherent flaws like poor character while excusing one's own similar mistakes as circumstantially driven, reflecting intellectual dishonesty and harsh judgments of others. Practicing empathy by imagining oneself in another's situation when they err rather than instantly condemning can mitigate attribution bias, as can conscious self-reflection on whether situational factors influenced missteps to avoid reflexively blaming personalities and moral failings of oneself or others. Overcoming the attribution bias tendency to see faults in others' actions but situational causation for one's own requires consciously fighting the double standard with perspective-taking and self-examination before rushing to assign blame.

·   ·   ·

Conformity Bias

Conformity bias causes people to agree with group behaviors or opinions despite privately disagreeing, stemming from an unconscious desire to gain acceptance and avoid social rejection or judgment even when acting counter to one's principles. Overcoming conformity bias requires conscious self-reflection on personal beliefs and critical evaluation of majority positions as an individual prior to going along with the group view or action. Promoting diversity of thought and rewarding those who respectfully challenge rather than blindly conform to the group's stance can reduce conformity bias, especially for those in leadership roles.

Beauty Bias

Beauty bias causes people to unconsciously judge others' capabilities and personalities based on physical attractiveness, manifesting in better treatment of those deemed attractive or worse treatment of those viewed as unattractive according to societal beauty standards. Recognizing beauty bias within oneself involves identifying assumptions made about new acquaintances' competencies, interests or behaviors solely because of very positive or negative assessments of their looks. Overcoming beauty bias requires conscious effort to evaluate people's qualities like intelligence based on their actual merits rather than presumed tendencies correlated to appearance, focusing on proven performance rather than perceptions.

Gender Bias

Gender bias manifests in discriminatory attitudes, assumptions, language, and unfair treatment towards others based solely on their gender rather than individual merits, perpetuating harmful stereotypes. Overcoming gender bias requires consciously using gender-neutral language, questioning reflexive judgments based on gender, and truly listening with an open mind when others share experiences of bias or mistreatment because of gender. Challenging ingrained stereotypical beliefs about what men or women should be like or do and instead evaluating people's capabilities and interests as individuals can help mitigate biased behaviors rooted in societal prejudice regarding gender.

Ageism

Ageism involves making biased assumptions about people's abilities, interests, or worth based solely on their age, whether they are young or old, perpetuating harmful stereotypes across generations. Combating ageism requires consciously evaluating people's competence, perspectives, and value as individuals rather than by blanket stereotypes, along with speaking out against age discrimination publicly and privately when observed. Seeking out friendships and mentorships across age groups helps challenge ingrained prejudice by highlighting the diversity within generations and universal human needs we all share regardless of age.

Contrast Effect

The contrast effect is a cognitive bias where comparing two options causes subjective perceptions of each to be shifted, such as when an outfit seems more professional because it's next to a sloppy one or a job candidate appears less impressive interviewed after a stellar applicant. Overcoming contrast effect bias requires consciously judging people or things on objective, isolated criteria rather than stacked side-by-side comparisons which subtly influence subjective opinions, so taking breaks between assessments or intentionally focusing analysis on facts rather than contextual impressions can reduce this tendency. Deciding independently of recent contrasts, whether in clothing, coworkers, or significant comparisons, leads to more accurate appraisals less affected by relative distortions with other options.

 A note from the trenches

When our marketing team was developing a new promotional campaign targeted at millennials, there was strong bias amongst some team members about what would appeal to that demographic. Several senior executives were convinced millennials would only engage with flashy digital content and scoffed at suggestions to incorporate print mailers. They selectively presented data showing declining print readership as proof.

However, when one of our younger associates presented focus group feedback showing that personalized, creative mailers actually captured significant attention, the executives dismissed it. Despite acknowledging the focus group limitations, they continued demanding an exclusively digital campaign, only wanting data that aligned with their preconceived notions.

Their confirmation bias closed them off to a hybrid approach that could have improved results by expanding channels. Unfortunately, the all-digital campaign performed poorly, but rather than reevaluating, the executives blamed external factors. This showed how bias can perpetuate continued poor decisions when people filter information to confirm their existing worldview. Overcoming that bias sooner could have led to a more effective strategy.

- RS

Lack of Critical Thinking Skills

Many instances of illogical decision-making can be attributed to a lack of critical thinking skills. Education systems and society often focus more on imparting knowledge rather than teaching individuals how to think critically. By emphasizing the importance of analytical thinking, we can empower individuals to make more thoughtful choices. Promoting courses or workshops on critical thinking, logic, and problem-solving can be beneficial in addressing this gap.

COUNTERING THE STUPIDITY EFFECTIVELY

Armed with knowledge, it's time to explore practical strategies to counter stupid decision-making. From gentle persuasion to subtle redirection, we'll explore various approaches and techniques designed to maximize your chances of achieving positive outcomes in the face of overwhelming irrationality. I know this sounds like a lot, but once you understand the basics, you will be able to tackle this effectively. It only requires a small amount of learning.

Communicate effectively

Engaging in meaningful and respectful dialogue with decision-makers is crucial for challenging their flawed decisions. Using clear and concise language, presenting well-reasoned arguments and evidence, and avoiding personal attacks can increase the likelihood of them considering alternative viewpoints. It is also important to provide them with an opportunity to voice their concerns and be heard, as this can help build trust and receptiveness to new ideas. Trust is going to be important when starting this journey, as you are required to be a leader to those who aren't necessarily easily led.

 A note from the trenches

I can still vividly remember the executive team's incredibly short-sighted decision to slash our marketing budget by 75% to save money. As the head of marketing, I knew that such a move would drastically lower the profile of the brand and make it harder to attract new customers.

I teamed up with the head of sales and we formed an alliance since he shared my worries about stunting growth trajectories. We advocated for a system of performance-based budget reallocation instead of random cuts. Subtly rubbing the CEO's ego, I argued these cuts would make us less competitive in our field. I also put together renderings showing how modest cuts and improved advertising targeting might keep awareness high and achieve objectives.

I presented the concept with evidence and reasoning in a follow-up meeting. The executive group understood their error after my presentation. In the end, the CEO told me that my plan did a good job of balancing expansion with cost management.

Through building relationships, recognizing motives and applying compelling data, I reversed a hasty decision that would have been disastrous to the organization. Irrational reaction was overcome by reasoned strategy.

- YB

Appeal to empathy

Sometimes, highlighting the potential impact of a stupid decision on others can evoke empathy and ignite a more compassionate response. By illustrating the consequences their actions may have on individuals or communities, decision-makers may reconsider their initial stance. Using storytelling or real-life case studies can create emotional connections and foster understanding. In a subtle way, this provides the space for growth and change in a way that is positive and comfortable for all. The decision-maker needs to trust their own choices in order to make them confidently.

Present viable alternatives

Offering practical and logical alternatives provides decision-makers with viable options that align with their goals while avoiding the pitfalls of their original course. By providing well-researched alternatives and highlighting the potential benefits, we can guide decision-makers toward more rational choices. It is essential to present these alternatives in a comprehensive and compelling manner, addressing potential concerns and showcasing their feasibility.

LEARNING FROM STUPID DECISIONS

Believe it or not, stupid decisions can teach us valuable lessons. Explore how you can extract wisdom from these situations, learning how *not* to repeat history. By turning ignorance into insight, you'll not only grow personally but also develop a better understanding of human behavior. There is no more valuable lesson to learn in this world.

Reflect on personal biases

As I mentioned before, biases play a major role in decision making. Stupid decisions made by others can serve as a mirror reflecting our own biases and flaws. Reflecting on our own decision-making processes can help us identify and address any hidden biases, making us more aware and better equipped to avoid similar pitfalls. Engaging in regular self-reflection and seeking feedback from trusted individuals can contribute to personal growth and improved decision-making.

Encourage self-improvement

Stupid decisions made by others can inspire personal growth and self-improvement. By actively seeking lessons in every situation, we can harness these experiences and use them as opportunities for growth. Analyze the consequences of the stupid decision and identify what went wrong and why. Reflect on how you can avoid making similar mistakes in the future by developing better decision-making strategies, increasing your knowledge and skills, and enhancing your critical thinking abilities.

Cultivate resilience

Dealing with stupid decision-making can be immensely frustrating and disheartening. However, it is essential to cultivate resilience and not let these situations demoralize you. View them as challenges to overcome and opportunities for personal growth. Learn to bounce back from setbacks, adapt to difficult circumstances, and maintain a positive mindset. Resilience will not only help you navigate the world of stupidity, but it will also strengthen your overall ability to handle obstacles in life.

CREATING A CULTURE OF RATIONALITY

While we may not be able to eradicate stupidity entirely, we can strive to create a culture of rationality that fosters logical decision-making and critical thinking. By advocating for evidence-based approaches, nurturing open-mindedness, and promoting education on rational thinking, we can contribute to a society that values logic and reason. There is no better platform for success.

Promote Critical Thinking Education

Recognize the importance of critical thinking skills and advocate for its inclusion in the workplace. Incorporate courses and workshops that teach employees how to think critically, solve problems, and make informed decisions. By equipping your team with these skills, we can empower them to navigate the complexities of our work environment with rationality and discernment.

Lead by example

Be a role model for rational decision-making by consistently showing logical thinking, critical analysis, and thoughtful consideration of information. Show others that reasoned approaches yield better outcomes and encourage them to adopt similar strategies. By leading by example, you can inspire others to prioritize logic over irrational impulses.

In the realm of stupid decision-making, it's essential to navigate with patience, empathy, and a solid grasp of logic. By understanding the different levels of the stupidity spectrum, analyzing the factors contributing to irrational choices, countering stupidity effectively, maintaining your sanity amidst the chaos, and learning from these situations, you can emerge unscathed, armed with wisdom and resilience. Let's embrace the challenges and uncertainties of navigating a world where logic sometimes takes a detour and strive to shape a culture that values rationality above all else.

Before you move on, let's recap:

1. Recognize different levels of stupidity on a spectrum, from mild confusion to utter foolishness.

Action step

Assess where poor decisions fall on the spectrum to determine the best response.

2. Understand the role of emotional reasoning and cognitive biases driving stupid choices.

Action step

Identify specific biases at play and appeal to logic and facts.

3. Communicate respectfully with well-reasoned arguments and data.

Action step

Present simple information focused on potential impact and alternatives.

4. Learn from others' mistakes through self-reflection.

Action step

Analyze the situation to extract lessons applicable to your own decision-making.

· · ·

5. Cultivate resilience and stay solution-focused.

Action step

View dealing with stupidity as an opportunity to grow while maintaining composure.

CHAPTER 7

SURVIVING MEETINGS: A BEGINNER'S GUIDE

A h, the dreaded meeting. A necessary evil that often feels like a vortex of wasted time and endless circular discussions. Yes, you're probably right in thinking that this meeting really should've been an email. The types of people mentioned in this book are the very reason it could never be as simple as an email. A bummer, I know. In this chapter, I'm going to equip you with an arsenal of tools and techniques needed to emerge unscathed from these soul-sucking sessions.

Prepare Yourself Mentally

Before entering the meeting room, take a deep breath and brace yourself for what lies ahead. Remind yourself that this is simply a test of your patience and endurance. Mental fortitude is key. Visualize yourself as a warrior, ready to navigate the treacherous waters of corporate conversations. And remember, it will eventually end. I promise.

Meetings are often seen as necessary evils, but they can also be valuable opportunities to share ideas, collaborate, and align goals. By shifting your mindset from one of dread to one of curiosity and possibility, you will open yourself up to the potential benefits that meetings can bring. Consider reframing meetings as opportunities for growth, learning, and networking. This mental preparation sets the stage for a more positive and productive experience.

Sharpen Your Listening Skills

In a room full of ignorance, it's vital that you focus. Yes, even if someone is rehashing a point for the ninth time. Sometimes, beneath the layers of repetition, a diamond of wisdom waits to be unearthed. Train yourself to filter out the noise and focus on the essence of the discussion.

Listening is a powerful tool in the art of effective communication. It allows us to understand diverse perspectives, identify key insights, and build stronger relationships. Practice active listening by giving your full attention to the speaker, avoiding interruptions, and asking clarifying questions when needed. By truly engaging with the content being shared, you can contribute meaningfully to the conversation and show your attentiveness and respect for others. In the end, there is no way to avoid meetings. Your best bet is to learn how to make them more beneficial to you.

Master the Art of Nodding and Smiling

There will be moments when you have no idea what's being said or why it's being said. In these instances, nodding and smiling will become your lifeline. It gives the illusion of engagement while your mind wanders to more productive thoughts, like what you'll have for lunch. But remember, moderation is key. If you nod too much, you might be mistaken for an agreeable fool. Or it might give away the fact that you're barely paying any attention.

Nonverbal communication plays a significant role in meetings. Nodding and smiling can create a positive atmosphere, encourage others to share their thoughts, and convey an engaged and attentive demeanor. When you genuinely do not understand, consider politely seeking clarification or offering a fresh perspective. Authenticity and thoughtfulness are valued more than mindless agreement.

Cultivate the Poker Face

It's not uncommon for mind-bogglingly stupid suggestions to be thrown around during meetings. Your facial expression should resemble that of a professional poker player. Maintain a neutral expression, no matter how much you want to roll your eyes or bang your head against the table. Deep breaths, control your impulses and project an aura of composed intelligence.

Balancing expressing your thoughts and maintaining professional decorum is essential. While it's tempting to react emotionally or visibly, and display frustration, doing so undermines effective communication and teamwork. By cultivating a poker face, you create a sense of professionalism and open the door for more constructive dialogue. Remember, it's not about suppressing your thoughts or ideas, but about finding the right time and approach to share them productively.

 A note from the trenches

It was only my third week into my new job when I attended my first major strategy meeting. I entered the conference room brimming with energy and ideas to contribute. However, my enthusiasm quickly deflated as the discussion unfolded. The marketing director unveiled a new campaign targeting "wealthy retirees," relying on outdated stereotypes and assumptions. When I pointed out more nuanced data on this demographic's values and priorities, my input was dismissed with a chuckle.

Over the next hour, one impractical idea after another was raised without being challenged. Each time I posed thoughtful objections or alternatives grounded in consumer research, they were batted down or outright ignored. The absurdity reached new heights when the VP suggested targeting "active elders" through print newspaper ads.

That meeting sparked simmering frustration at the collective failure to leverage data and critical thinking. My early excitement about bringing a fresh perspective turned to disillusionment at the organization's mediocrity and bias against new ideas. Driving actual change here would be an uphill battle —a reality that initially felt hopeless yet eventually inspired me to equip others facing this bureaucratic madness.

- GJ

Prepare Your Exit Strategy

Meetings often run longer than necessary or devolve into tangents that kill any productivity for the rest of the day. Plan your escape route in advance. Position yourself close to the door, ready to make a swift exit as soon as you spot an opportunity. Use subtle body language to signal your readiness to contribute, then gracefully excuse yourself, citing "time constraints" and "urgent matters."

While it's important to be respectful of allocated meeting times, it's equally crucial to prioritize your own productivity and well-being. Planning an exit strategy doesn't mean avoiding responsibilities or disengaging from the discussion; rather, it enables you to manage your time effectively and maintain a healthy work-life balance. Always be considerate of others, communicate your availability, and ensure you fulfill any commitments or contributions expected from you before exiting. As far as possible, communicate your time constraints ahead of time. That way, should you need to mention it as an exit strategy, it does not surprise those in attendance.

If you're still feeling stuck, here is some knowledge that has helped me through:

Strategies to steer conversations and reign in tangents during meetings (*MindTools | Home*, n.d.):

- Ask clarifying questions: If the conversation goes off on a tangent, politely interject with a question that steers things back on track, such as "How does this tie back to the agenda topic we were discussing?" or "Could you explain how that point relates to the goal of this meeting?"
- Summarize and transition: Provide a brief summary of the tangent discussion, then use transitional phrases to redirect. For example, "We've thoroughly explored X idea. Moving back to the original agenda…"
- Refer back to agenda/objectives: Explicitly redirect to the pre-defined goals for the meeting by saying something like "To ensure we achieve the objectives outlined in the agenda, let's table that thought and return to discussing Y initiative."
- Time checks: Note how much time has elapsed in the meeting and subtly remind participants to be conscious

of staying on schedule. For example, "We have 15 minutes remaining, so let's focus on accomplishing Z before we adjourn."

Document Everything

In the realm of absurdity, documentation is your armor. Keep a detailed record of all the bizarre ideas and nonsensical statements that can occur during meetings. Documenting key points, decisions, and action items is a valuable practice in meetings. By providing a clear record of discussions and outcomes, you ensure accountability and alignment among participants. Taking accurate notes allows you to refer to specific details, recall agreements, and track progress. It shows professionalism and attentiveness, as well as positions you as a valuable resource when others need to recollect or refer to the meeting's content. This serves as a subtle way for you to take the lead when necessary, managing the trajectory of the meeting.

Find Allies in the Room

Seek out fellow intelligent beings in the room who share your pain. Bonding over shared frustration can help ease the agony of the meeting. These allies can provide comic relief during the most trying of times and serve as your support system in the battle against mind-numbing meetings.

Building connections and fostering relationships within the meeting context can lead to greater collaboration and innovation. Identifying like-minded individuals who share your frustrations or goals can provide a sense of camaraderie and support. Together, you can find creative ways to navigate the challenges and potentially spark positive change within the meeting culture. Remember, finding allies is not about engaging in negativity, but embracing the power of collaboration and shared experiences. If you've taken on the chance to instill change, then they can help you. Consistency will always be key, and the more people are on board, the better.

Develop a Sense of Humor

Laughter, they say, is the best medicine. In meetings, it's a survival technique. As we touched upon in a previous chapter, finding humor in the ridiculousness of it all will go a long way. A well-timed joke or a clever pun can lighten the mood and relieve tension while providing you with a much-needed sense of control. Contrary to popular belief, laughing easily does not make you look nervous. Laughing easily gives an air of confidence. The trick is, not to laugh when it is inappropriate.

Humor has a remarkable ability to foster creativity, relieve stress, and enhance communication. In meetings where tensions and pressures can run high, injecting a dose of lightheartedness can create a more inclusive and enjoyable atmosphere. Humor also helps to break down barriers, enabling more open and honest conversations. However, it is crucial to strike the right balance and be mindful of the context and cultural sensitivities. Respect and inclusivity should always remain at the core of any attempt at humor.

Remember, these meetings shall come to pass. By employing these strategies, you'll not only survive but also maintain a semblance of sanity amid the chaos. Turn the dreaded meeting into a personal conquer! A game in which your only opponent is the person you were in the last meeting. Now brace yourself, for the meeting room awaits. Good luck and may your survival skills be forever sharp!

Points to remember:

1. Prepare mentally to withstand frustration and test your patience.

Action step

Visualize yourself as a warrior ready to navigate challenges.

2. Sharpen listening skills to identify insights amid repetition.

Action step

Filter noise and focus on the essence of discussions.

3. Master the art of nodding and smiling to feign engagement.

Action step

Convey positivity but seek clarification if genuinely confused.

4. Cultivate a poker face to conceal reactions to absurdity.

Action step

Control impulses and maintain a neutral, professional demeanor.

5. Plan an exit strategy to leave unproductive meetings.

Action step

Politely excuse yourself when possible citing other priorities.

CHAPTER 8
THE ART OF STEALTH: HIDING YOUR FRUSTRATION IN PLAIN SIGHT

F rustration can be an all-consuming emotion when you find yourself surrounded by stupidity. The urge to scream, pull your hair out, or simply walk away can become overpowering. In order to maintain a semblance of professionalism and sanity, mastering the art of stealth becomes crucial. Responding emotionally to frustration might make you difficult to work with, which is the last thing you want. It's tough to manage this, but it is always beneficial and makes for a better day.

The Poker Face

As we proposed in an earlier chapter, employ the poker face. In order to master this, you must first understand the psychology behind it. A poker face is not just a blank expression; it is a carefully crafted mask that hides your inner turmoil. Start by analyzing your own facial expressions in front of a mirror. Notice how subtle changes in your eyebrows, mouth, and eyes can convey emotions. Practice maintaining a neutral expression, slightly raising your eyebrows, and relaxing your facial muscles to create a calm demeanor. This will give you an air of control and mystery, disguising any frustration that may be boiling beneath the surface. If you're still stuck, search the internet for body language courses. Mastering the finer details of this can help aid your poker face into an unshakable thing.

Strategic Vents

While it's important to hide your frustration from colleagues, it is equally vital to release that pent-up tension in a healthy and constructive manner. Seek out trusted colleagues who share your struggles and can empathize. A wise mentor of mine once told me to only vent to those above you, never to your subordinates, as this could create doubt and negativity. Arrange discreet venting sessions during lunch breaks or after work, where you can collectively let off steam and commiserate about the insanity around you. These sessions can serve as a cathartic release, allowing you to recharge and return to work with a renewed sense of calm and focus. However, remember that moderation is key, as excessive venting can easily turn into an unproductive cycle of negativity. Positivity will always breed more positivity. The same goes for negativity. Avoid it as much as possible.

If you really need to vent and your poker face is at risk, here are some ideas for finding healthy outlets to vent frustration ("Control Anger Before It Controls You," 2023):

Exercise or physical activity
Go for a run, hit the gym, play sports. Physical exertion releases endorphins and relieves stress.

Listen to music
Find some upbeat music that matches your mood or play calming music to relax.

Write in a journal
Pour out your feelings by writing them down. This can clarify your thoughts.

Talk to a friend or mentor
Vent to someone you trust who can listen without judgment.

Engage in a hobby
Lose yourself in a hobby like painting, woodworking, or gardening that takes your mind off work.

Volunteer in your community
Contribute your time to a cause which can boost your mood and purpose.

Seek counseling or therapy
Speak to a professional therapist to gain coping strategies.

Self-Regulation Techniques

When frustration threatens to bubble to the surface, it is crucial to have self-regulation techniques at your disposal. Take deep, slow breaths to activate the body's relaxation response. Count to ten, allowing yourself a moment to pause and regain composure. Visualize yourself in a peaceful environment, such as a serene beach or a tranquil forest, to shift your focus away from the immediate source of frustration. Engaging in regular physical exercise, meditation, or mindfulness practices can also help to ease stress and improve emotional regulation. These techniques not only preserve your sanity but also equip you with the resilience needed to navigate challenging situations with grace. Make things easier on yourself by adopting small practices to get you through your frustration.

Seek Intellectual Stimulus

In order to maintain your own intellectual sanity amidst the intellectual chaos, seek out opportunities to engage in stimulating activities outside of work. Join book clubs, attend seminars, or pursue personal hobbies that challenge and expand your intellect. Surround yourself with like-minded individuals who appreciate the depths of intellectual discourse. These activities will provide a much-needed respite from the mind-numbing intellect of your co-workers, allowing you to recharge and reconnect with the fulfillment that comes from pursuing knowledge and understanding. It helps to separate work life from personal life, giving you a reason to get through each day. Finding others in the workplace with similar interests, or interests that intrigue you, can provide breaks from your focus in a healthy and brain-nourishing manner.

Practice Empathy

Though it may be challenging, practicing empathy is essential when dealing with intellectually challenging individuals. This is a point that comes up regularly throughout this book, as I'm sure you have noticed. That is because it needs to be consistent throughout your efforts. Recognize that everyone has their own strengths and weaknesses, and some individuals may excel in areas where they struggle intellectually. Put yourself in their shoes, considering the context they come from, their upbringing, or external factors that may contribute to their shortcomings in certain areas. Remember that intelligence comes in various forms, and what may seem obvious to you may require more effort for others to grasp. Cultivating empathy can help you find common ground, foster healthier relationships, and navigate working dynamics more effectively. Understanding why someone is how they are can help you accommodate those weaknesses when dealing with them, ultimately streamlining every interaction positively.

Continuous Learning

Embrace the mindset of continuous learning to counteract frustrations caused by intellectual disparities. Foster a growth mindset that values the learning process over immediate results. Approach each interaction as an opportunity to grow and expand your own knowledge. Stay curious, ask questions, and challenge yourself to seek information and perspectives that you may not have considered before. Encourage curiosity within yourself and others, promoting a culture of learning in your workplace. By focusing on personal growth, you can redirect your frustration into a motivation for personal and professional development, further strengthening your own intellect and resilience. There is much to learn out there, embrace it.

Set Boundaries

Maintaining a healthy work-life balance is crucial to minimize frustration. Set clear boundaries between your professional and personal life, ensuring that work-related stress does not encroach on your personal time. Designate specific hours for work-related tasks, and outside of those hours, disconnect and engage in activities that bring you joy and relaxation. Establishing healthy boundaries will help protect your mental well-being and preserve your energy for activities outside of work.

Remember, you are not defined solely by your job, and it is essential to maintain a well-rounded life in order to thrive both professionally and personally. By embracing the art of stealth and aligning yourself with these strategies, you can navigate the challenges of working with the intellectually challenged while preserving your professional demeanor and personal well-being. Emphasize empathy, continuous learning, and self-care to not only manage frustrations effectively but also thrive in a potentially challenging environment. Never underestimate the indomitable power of your intellect and resilience.

In summary, this is how you maintain stealth and resilience:

1. Craft a poker face by controlling facial expressions and projecting calm.

Action step

Practice in the mirror analyzing subtle emotional cues.

2. Vent constructively to trusted colleagues in discreet settings.

Action step

Arrange occasional venting sessions during breaks to release tension.

3. Employ self-regulation techniques like deep breathing and visualization.

Action step

Mentally transport yourself to a peaceful setting when frustrated.

4. Pursue intellectually stimulating hobbies and connections beyond work.

Action step

Join book clubs or seminars aligned with personal interests.

5. Set clear boundaries between work and personal life.

Action step

Disconnect after work hours and spend time on joyful activities.

CHAPTER 9
THE POWER OF SARCASM: HOW TO USE IT WITHOUT GETTING FIRED

Sarcasm is a double-edged sword. When wielded properly, it can diffuse tension, provide comic relief, and even offer a subtle critique of the absurdities we encounter in the workplace. It will also make you feel better. Sarcasm has a way of allowing a brief emotional release, without becoming negative. However, when used inappropriately or excessively, it can create misunderstandings, hurt feelings, and potentially jeopardize your professional reputation. In this chapter, we'll discuss the art of sarcasm, exploring its nuances, benefits, and potential pitfalls while providing practical tips on how to master it without crossing the line.

Know Your Audience

Understanding your audience is crucial when using sarcasm. While some people embrace humorous banter, others may find it offensive or disruptive. There are people out there, among us, who take everything seriously. And I mean *everything*. Those people will almost certainly not respond well to sarcasm. Before injecting sarcasm into your conversations, take a moment to assess your audience's personality, communication style, and level of familiarity with you. Are they receptive to humor, or do they prefer direct and literal communication? Are they familiar with your wit and sarcasm, or is this their first interaction with your sense of humor? Understanding your audience's preferences and levels of sensitivity will not only help you gauge the appropriate use of sarcasm but also build stronger connections and promote effective communication.

Timing Is Everything

Sarcasm is most effective when used sparingly and at the right moment. The key lies in discerning the appropriate timing for its deployment. Avoid using sarcasm during serious or delicate discussions, as it can undermine trust, diminish the significance of important matters, or derail productive conversations. Instead, reserve sarcasm for lighthearted conversations, casual interactions, or when the situation calls for a humorous touch.

Tone and Delivery

Mastering the art of sarcasm involves honing your tone and delivery. It's crucial to strike a balance between exaggeration and subtlety. Employing a playful tone, a raised eyebrow, or a slight smirk can signal your intent and help distinguish sarcasm from seriousness. However, be mindful that your nonverbal cues are clear enough to avoid confusion or offense. Practice your delivery to ensure that your sarcasm is received as intended and always be open to adjusting your delivery style based on feedback and the reactions you receive.

Contextual Awareness

While sarcasm works in certain contexts, it may not be suitable for all situations. Consider the environment and the nature of your professional relationships when deciding to employ sarcasm. Are you interacting with coworkers, superiors, or clients? Be aware of the power dynamics and understand the prevailing norms within your workplace culture. Tailor your sarcasm to fit the context, and when in doubt, err on the side of caution. Being mindful of the appropriateness of sarcasm will help you navigate the fine line between humor and insensitivity.

Balance with Positivity

To maintain a healthy and productive work environment, it's important to balance sarcasm and positivity. While sarcasm can be a powerful tool, excessive or negative sarcasm can create a toxic atmosphere or damage relationships. Balancing sarcasm with positive reinforcement, genuine compliments, and supportive remarks will ensure that you are seen as a constructive and collaborative team player. Pairing sarcasm with kindness and empathy can further enhance your ability to connect with others and promote a healthier work culture.

Address Misunderstandings Swiftly

Despite your best efforts, misunderstandings can still occur when using sarcasm. If someone misinterprets your sarcastic remark, don't brush it off or assume they should have understood your intent. Address the misunderstanding swiftly and directly. Clarify your statement, explain your intended sarcasm, and ensure that you reestablish clear and respectful communication. This proactive step can preserve relationships, prevent further confusion, and contribute to a more cohesive and understanding work environment. This will probably only happen once in each instance. The moment you clarify any misunderstanding, the person on the receiving end will understand the next time to revert to sarcasm, and likely not take it so personally.

Gauge the Organizational Culture

Every organization has its unique culture and communication norms. What may be acceptable and appreciated in one workplace may not be in another. Observe your colleagues and superiors to gain a sense of what is tolerated and appreciated in terms of sarcasm. Adapt your communication style to align with the organizational culture, which will help you navigate the fine line between wit and insensitivity. Being attuned to the organizational culture not only shows your adaptability but also shows your ability to effectively communicate and build rapport within the specific framework of your workplace. This makes you pleasant to work with, no matter where you find yourself.

Sarcasm, when used appropriately and judiciously, can inject humor and lightness into the work environment, fostering camaraderie and promoting effective communication. By understanding your audience, being mindful of context, and practicing effective delivery, you can harness the power of sarcasm without crossing the line. Embrace sarcasm as a valuable communication tool, and let it enhance your professional interactions while keeping your sense of humor intact. With each witty remark, you can navigate challenging situations, build bridges, and create a more enjoyable work environment for yourself and those around you.

Just in case you forget:

1. Know your audience and gauge if they appreciate sarcasm.

Action step

Assess their personality and preferences before using sarcasm.

2. Use sarcasm sparingly and appropriately.

Action step

Avoid sarcasm in serious or sensitive conversations and inter-actions.

3. Master tone and delivery for clear intent.

Action step

Practice subtle verbal and nonverbal cues like a playful tone and raised eyebrow.

4. Consider context and professional relationships.

Action step

Tailor sarcasm to align with workplace culture and dynamics with different groups.

5. Balance sarcasm with positivity.

Action step

Pair humor with genuine praise, kindness, and empathy to build trust.

CHAPTER 10

LIGHT AT THE END OF THE CUBICLE: ESCAPING THE STUPIDITY TRAP

I n the depths of the corporate world, where intellect often takes a back seat to mediocrity, it's easy to feel suffocated and trapped in an environment plagued by stupidity. However, beneath the shadow cast by mindless coworkers and soul-draining tasks, there is a glimmer of hope - a way to break free from this intellectual purgatory and embark on a path towards enlightenment and fulfillment. There is a method to push through and survive it with your humor and sanity intact. Guidance exists that can lead you through the stupid chaos and get you to the end of your day, unscathed. You can do it. Yes, you can.

Assess Your Options

As you are enveloped by the fog of stupidity, take a step back and engage in a self-reflective exercise. Ask yourself the tough questions: Are you truly happy in your current job? Is there potential for personal growth and development? Understanding your options is the first crucial step toward liberation.

Before making any drastic decisions, consider the consequences and implications they might have on your financial stability, personal relationships, and overall well-being. Reflect on your core values, passions, and strengths. Explore alternative career paths, industries, or even entrepreneurial ventures that align with your authentic self. Research the potential challenges, opportunities, and market demands associated with each option to make an informed decision. No matter what you do, you do not need to feel stuck in your job. All you need is some patience, and some resilience. If leaving is what you need to do, then you can take the necessary steps. But be certain of where you're going, and the risk you're taking first.

Build Your Skill Set

While swimming in a sea of stupidity, seize every encounter as an opportunity for personal and professional growth. Embrace challenging projects, however nonsensical they may appear at first glance. Recognize that perseverance and resilience are essential for meaningful growth.

Seek additional training, seminars, or courses that can equip you with new skills and knowledge. Identify areas where you can develop expertise or explore emerging trends within your industry. By continuously expanding your skill set, you stay relevant and adaptable in a rapidly evolving professional landscape. In the meantime, you'll discover new hobbies or passions and find a further fulfillment in your day. Learning will always result in success.

 A note from the trenches

I once worked for a company that incentivized employees to continue learning and growing. They offered generous financial rewards to those who read books from a recommended reading list curated by leadership. The list spanned diverse topics, from psychology and mindset to sales and marketing strategies, and as we read these books aligned with our interests during our personal time, we expanded our skills and thinking. The company benefited from more informed, educated team members. This creative program enabled employees to earn extra compensation while becoming more valuable contributors. It struck an excellent balance between rewarding employees and cultivating talent organically. I found it motivating to get paid to read content that simultaneously enhanced my capabilities. This win-win initiative kept employees engaged and equipped the company with an ever-evolving talent pool.

-MS

Cultivate a mindset of curiosity and continuous learning in your environment. Engage in self-directed learning, read books from diverse genres, and explore topics outside your immediate field of expertise. This broad perspective will enhance your problem-solving abilities and deepen your understanding of the world around you.

If you don't know where to start, here are some ways to improve your skill set (Panel, 2021):

1. Take online courses
2. Sponsor conferences and seminars
3. Promote cross-training and job shadowing
4. Offer tuition reimbursement programs
5. Provide stretch assignment opportunities

6. Develop in-house mentorship programs
7. Host regular training workshops
8. Create skills development plans
9. Invest in new technologies and software
10. Reward continuing education and growth

Expand Your Network

Building a robust and diverse professional network can be the life raft that carries you away from the stupidity trap. Attend industry events, join professional associations, and engage in networking activities to connect with like-minded individuals who share your vision and values.

Networking is not just about collecting business cards or making superficial connections; it's about building genuine, mutually beneficial relationships. Seek out mentors who can guide you on your path to freedom, providing invaluable insights, connections, and support. Invest time in nurturing these relationships and offering your own expertise and assistance in return.

Leverage the power of social media platforms to expand your network beyond physical boundaries. Engage with industry thought leaders, join relevant online communities, and take part in discussions. The virtual realm has opened endless possibilities to connect, collaborate, and learn from professionals worldwide. Use it to your benefit and use it wisely.

Develop an Exit Strategy

Escaping the stupidity trap requires careful planning and calculated action. Set specific goals and create a timeline for your escape. Identify milestones, such as acquiring certain skills or experiences, building a financial safety net, or establishing alternative income streams.

Craft an exit strategy that aligns with your career aspirations and personal circumstances. Consider potential roadblocks, such as fear of change, financial constraints, or other obligations, and develop contingency plans to overcome them. Seek advice from professionals in your desired field, conduct thorough research, and consult with those who have successfully made similar transitions. Use the network you have built for support, that is why that network exists.

Remaining flexible and adaptable along the way will allow you to make strategic decisions that propel you closer to the elusive freedom you seek. Embrace calculated risks and view setbacks as valuable learning experiences that enable you to refine your approach and move forward stronger than before.

 A note from the trenches

> I finally had enough after years of being stifled by an incompetent and bureaucratic work culture that was poisonous to my health. Even though I was terrified of leaving my secure corporate career, I longed to make a difference by playing to my skills.
>
> After giving it some serious thought, I realized that teaching has always been my calling. What rekindled my passion was taking on the role of a weekend tutor for disadvantaged youngsters as a volunteer. I was able to get a job as a substitute teacher at a nearby school not long after. I had to take a pay cut at first, but the ability to make a difference in the lives of young people gave me purpose and excitement every day.
>
> My first year of teaching full-time was fruitful. The satisfaction I get from showing the way for the next

generation has made the poisonous job seem like a distant memory. This change was fraught with uncertainty, but I overcame it by directing my professional life that was true to who I am. Now I work in an environment that challenges me intellectually and allows my skills to flourish.

- CL

Pursue Passion Projects

While you may not have the luxury of escaping stupidity entirely in your current job, you can preserve your sanity and find fulfillment by pursuing passion projects outside of work. Engage in activities or hobbies that ignite your passion and creativity.

Experiment with various artistic outlets, explore entrepreneurship in your spare time or engage in volunteer work that aligns with your values. These endeavors will provide a much-needed outlet, allowing you to express your authentic self and find joy amidst the chaos. Sometimes the answer is not to remove everything that doesn't work, but rather to add things that make it survivable.

As you immerse yourself in these projects, you may even discover hidden talents and possibilities that can reshape your trajectory. Consider the potential of turning your passion projects into viable career paths or side businesses. By aligning your work with your passions, you create an ecosystem that nourishes your intellectual, emotional, and creative needs. It is important to remember that you may come across stupid and frustrating people everywhere you go, but as you go toward the things you love, the stupid will feel less frustrating.

Take the Leap

Armed with knowledge, skills, and a burning desire for intellectual enlightenment, the time will come to take the final leap of faith. This pivotal moment demands conviction and bravery.

Put your carefully laid groundwork into motion and embark on your new journey. Whether it's starting your own business, switching careers, or finding a job in a more intellectually stimulating environment, trust in your abilities and let your passion guide you.

Be prepared for the challenges that may arise, for the path to freedom may not be smooth. Embrace the lessons, setbacks, and triumphs along the way as they forge you into a stronger, wiser individual. Cultivate resilience and adaptability, for they are the strengths that will carry you through uncertain times.

In the end, escaping the stupidity trap requires determination, perseverance, and resilience. Remember that enlightenment and fulfillment await those brave enough to pursue it. Shed the shackles of mediocrity, embrace your true potential, and soar toward the light at the end of the cubicle.

Don't forget what you've learned:

1. Reflect on your career fulfillment and explore alternative options aligned with your values.

Action step

Assess if your current role allows growth and conduct informational interviews.

2. View challenging situations as opportunities to build your skills.

Action step

Seek training and self-education to expand expertise.

3. Cultivate professional connections to find mentors and advice.

Action step

Attend conferences and networking events to meet like-minded individuals.

4. Craft a transition strategy with timelines based on acquiring skills and financial readiness.

Action step

Research the steps to change careers or start a business.

5. Pursue passion projects outside work as creative outlets.

Action step

Experiment with hobbies, volunteer work, or side businesses related to your interests.

FINAL WORDS

And so, we come to the end of our journey through the unconventional and absurd world of working with stupid people. Over the past chapters, we have braved the stormy seas of irrationality, forged new paths through the jungles of confusion, and emerged battle-hardened, yet triumphant.

Through vivid anecdotes, psychological insights, and practical strategies, I have aimed to shed light on the various species of workplace stupidity, the inner workings of the not-so-intelligent mind, and methods to counter, mitigate, and even harness stupidity for positive outcomes. We have seen that beneath the baffling behaviors often lie insecurity, stubbornness, and deep-rooted biases rather than sheer incapability. With the right mindset and communication approach, even the most seemingly hopeless cases of stupidity can be navigated through calmly.

The pages of this book have been filled with techniques for maintaining your composure, resolving conflicts diplomatically, presenting convincing arguments, and protecting your mental well-being amidst the chaos. You have learned the delicate art of subtle sarcasm, the power of emotional detachment, and the benefits of finding humor when all seems lost. Through memorable frameworks like the Spectrum of Stupidity, complex behaviors have been decoded into comprehensible patterns. The secrets of the oblivious mind have been exposed, paving the path to successful methods adapted to each type of absurdity.

While stupidity continues to dominate many workplaces, you are now equipped with the tools and wisdom to prevail. You can empower those around you with greater clarity while retaining your sanity. By focusing on the controllable—your reactions, mindset, communication style, and emotional regulation—you can achieve positive outcomes regardless of the irrational forces at play. The chaos and confusion may persist, but you will remain anchored in reason.

As you move forward, remember that enacting change starts with small, consistent steps. Set an example through your own rational thinking and patient guidance. Slowly foster a culture that values humility, critical thinking, and evidence-based decision making over brash reactivity. While the stupidity may never fully dissipate, collective effort can progressively shift workplace mindsets toward logic and reason.

You may occasionally stumble, experience setbacks, and want to abandon all hope. But I urge you to persist. Draw strength and inspiration from the mentors, allies, and like-minded connections you have forged along the way. Look back at obstacles already overcome with a sense of pride. For you now possess the resilience, wisdom, and clarity of mind to thrive while others remain trapped in the vortex of stupidity. You have emerged from the depths with heightened self-awareness and a newfound appreciation for the spectacle of absurdity.

The skills you have gained will serve you well regardless of where your professional journey leads. You can approach future challenges with calm determination, lead with compassionate authority, and de-escalate conflicts with eloquent diplomacy. Your expanded emotional intelligence and mental agility will empower you to handle difficult personalities and irrational agendas. You will become the eye of the hurricane—centered, responsive, and solution-focused while chaos unfolds around you. At the very least, this book will have taught you how *not* to be the stupid one in the group and that can be more beneficial than you could ever imagine.

And with that, I congratulate you! Few have the courage to confront stupidity head-on, with good humor and an open mind. But you chose the road less traveled, boldly venturing into uncharted territories of bewilderment. You now emerge wiser, with battle scars transformed into stories of courage. As you step back into the arena of absurdity, no matter the species of stupidity you encounter—be it the clueless, the biased, or the outright ridiculous—take comfort because you are now armed and ready. While the madness continues, go forth and unleash your inner Zen, logic, and rational resilience. The foundations have been laid for you to not only survive but thrive within the ecosystem of stupidity!

Special Request

If you have found my book to be helpful, I'd appreciate a review.

In doing so, you will help others who also find
themselves working with stupid people!

Thank you!

RESOURCES

Control anger before it controls you. (2023, November 3). *https://www.apa.org*. https://www.apa.org/topics/anger/control

Gould, W. R. (2023, June 20). *Signs of different types of biases and how to overcome each of them*. Verywell Mind. https://www.verywellmind.com/signs-of-bias-7501512

MindTools | Home. (n.d.). https://www.mindtools.com/pages/article/steering-meetings.htm

MSEd, K. C. (2022, November 10). *What is the confirmation bias?* Verywell Mind. https://www.verywellmind.com/what-is-a-confirmation-bias-2795024

Panel, E. (2021, October 22). Help employees continually develop their skills with these 16 strategies. *Forbes*. https://www.forbes.com/sites/forbeshumanresourcescouncil/2021/10/22/help-employees-continually-develop-their-skills-with-these-16-strategies/?sh=57f4f0c32673

Principia Scientific Intl. (2021, November 2). *The 5 basic laws of human stupidity, according to Cipolla | Principia Scientific Intl.* Principia Scientific Intl. | a Science-based Community.

https://principia-scientific.com/the-5-basic-laws-of-human-stupidity-according-to-cipolla/

Stanovich, K. (2009). *What intelligence tests miss: The Psychology of rational thought.* https://www.semanticscholar.org/paper/What-Intelligence-Tests-Miss%3A-The-Psychology-of-Stanovich/a6bef9a53b25f84cab8cc5339c2aea7f13f3765f

Made in United States
North Haven, CT
19 June 2024

53820934R00059